CONTENTS

St. John Bosco's famous dream about the two columns in the sea.

FOREWORD

Our age is starved for intimacy yet terrified of it. The majority of us live in quiet desperation, hungry for the touch of love and, above all for the touch of the love of God. Yet, such is our fear that the great majority of us also shy away from such contact. On the human level, that has been one contributor to the enormous frequency of failed relationships and shattered families, which in turn leads to a generation of children who grow up anesthetized to the possibility of real union with another.

But on the spiritual level as well, it has led to a safe and lonely view of God. A God who is the Force. A God who is not even a who (that's too intimate), but is merely a what: a vast, pervasive Something flowing through the ether like solar wind, requiring nothing but that we feel good about ourselves and administer weak salves of "self-affirmation" to our sadness.

This spiritual barricade to intimacy we have built is our comfort and our curse. It leaves us feeling safe from betrayal (and command) by God but also horribly alone as we sit consuming, filling up the void with TV and chocolate chip cookies.

The good news of Jesus Christ in the Eucharist is that we need not starve but can be filled. It is the shocking announcement that God, the Lover of our souls, is more than a vague Force. He is as concrete and specific as a kiss on the lips—or the nails through His hands and feet. It is the astonishingly good news that Love has come to *touch* us—physically and not just as a disembodied spirit—in the body, blood, spirit, soul and divinity of Jesus of Nazareth, the Word made flesh. Read this wonderful little book and see how such a wonder can be so. Share it with a friend so they can know too.

Then, taste and see!

—Mark P. Shea
Author of:
This is My Body: An Evangelical Discovers the Real Presence
By What Authority?: An Evangelical Discovers Catholic Tradition
Making Senses Out of Scripture: Reading the Bible Like the First Christians Did

INTRODUCTION

In 1862, St. John Bosco had a remarkable dream. He saw the Catholic Church as a mighty flagship in the midst of a great battle. Smaller enemy ships were bombarding it with books and pamphlets, bombs and cannons, and trying to ram it off course. At the same time, huge waves and fierce winds buffeted the flagship. At the helm, the Pope strained every muscle to steer his ship between two mighty columns in the sea. On the smaller column stood a statue of the Blessed Virgin Mary. On the other, far loftier column, was a large Host. In spite of all adversity, the Pope anchored the flagship to thick chains hanging from the two columns. At that, the enemy ships panicked and fled, while the wind and seas grew calm.

St. John Bosco explained that the Church will endure grave trials and persecutions. The Church's enemies will try their utmost to destroy her. But two things will preserve the Church in that hour: devotion to Mary and frequent Communion.

Bosco's vision illustrates that the greatest treasure in the Catholic Church is the Eucharist. In it, Jesus humbly assumes the appearance of bread and wine, proving His desire to be bodily connected to us.

Because it is Jesus Himself, the Eucharist is the heart of the Catholic faith. The new *Catechism of the Catholic Church* (hereafter, *CCC*) calls the Eucharist the "*source and summit of the Christian life*" and the "*sum and the summary of our faith*" (*CCC* 1324 and 1327). It's hard to imagine that any Catholic could misunderstand a central doctrine of his faith.

However, according to an alarming 1992 Gallup poll, the *majority* of Catholics are confused in their beliefs about Christ's presence in the Eucharist:

- **30%** believe they are really and truly receiving the body, blood, soul and divinity of the Lord Jesus Christ under the appearance of bread and wine.
- **29%** believe they are receiving bread and wine that *symbolize* the body and blood of Jesus.
- **10%** believe they receive *bread and wine* in which Jesus is also present.
- **24%** believe they are receiving what has become Christ's body and blood because of their *personal belief.*

Any well-informed Catholic will recognize that only the first option, chosen by the 30 percent, represents true Catholic teaching. The other options represent various Protestant beliefs. In other words, *nearly 70 percent of all Catholics in this country hold erroneous beliefs about Christ's presence in the Eucharist*!

The problem increases dramatically among younger Catholics. According to a more recent New York Times and CBS poll of Catholics *who attend Mass regularly*, the number who accept the Real Presence decreases as age decreases:

- Age 65 and over: **51%** believe in the Real Presence.
- Age 45–64: **37%** believe in the Real Presence.
- Age 30–44: **28%** believe in the Real Presence.
- Age 18–29: **17%** believe in the Real Presence.

70% of this last age group (18–29) believe the Eucharist is just a *symbol*. What does this say about how we are passing the faith on to our children? Only one teenager in six accepts the fundamental doctrine of the Real Presence! This loss of faith among young and old alike explains the tremendous lack of devotion, reverence, and appreciation so many Catholics show towards Holy Communion.

WHAT DOES THE CHURCH TEACH ABOUT THE EUCHARIST?

For nearly 2000 years, the Catholic Church has taught that Jesus Christ is really and truly present in the Eucharist. Under the appearance of bread and wine, Christ is completely present in His body and blood as well as His soul and divinity.

The moment the priest says the words of consecration—"This is my body" and "This is my blood"—God miraculously changes ordinary bread and wine into the body and blood of Christ. All the outward appearances and sensible qualities of the bread and wine remain. This transformation of substance is called *transubstantiation*. The substance of the bread and wine are changed into the substance of Christ's living body and blood. The bread and wine are gone, replaced by the real presence of Christ, while only their appearances remain.

> The moment the priest repeats Christ's words of consecration—"This is my body" and "This is my blood"— God miraculously changes ordinary bread and wine into the body and blood of Christ.

Jesus is present wholly and entirely in each of the Eucharistic elements (or species) as well as in each of its parts. The smallest sliver of the consecrated host or the tiniest drop from the chalice contains the whole Christ. We can receive Jesus under the form of bread alone, under the form of wine alone, or both together. In each case, we receive the same perfect sacrament, the same Jesus into our souls.

Because Jesus is truly present, we adore the Eucharist as God. That's why we genuflect (or bow deeply) before the tabernacle. That's why the Church reserves the consecrated hosts with such care. That's why the Church carries the consecrated hosts in processions and exposes them for solemn adoration.

Christ's presence in the Eucharist begins at the moment of consecration and lasts as long as the appearances of bread and wine remain. When a consecrated host is digested or dissolved and no longer has the qualities of bread, it is no longer Jesus.[1] When we receive Holy Communion, Jesus remains in our bodies for about 15 minutes. We should adore Him within us as long as He is sacramentally present. For a short time, we are living tabernacles of the all-holy God.

Because the Eucharist is our God and Savior Jesus Christ, we dare not receive Him in the state of mortal sin. To receive Jesus worthily, we must be in the state of grace. If we have committed a mortal sin, we cannot receive Holy Communion without first receiving absolution in the sacrament of confession.

[1] *CCC* 1377: "The Eucharistic presence of Christ begins at the moment of the consecration and endures as long as the Eucharistic species subsist."

We can't be indifferent about Christ's presence in the Eucharist. This issue separates Catholics from virtually all Protestants. If Christ is only *symbolically present* in the Eucharist, then Catholics are guilty of idolatry: worshiping mere bread and wine as God Himself. But if Christ is *really present* in the Eucharist, then most non-Catholics are guilty of not recognizing—or worse, denying and rejecting—their Lord and Savior in the Eucharist.

Both sides are obligated to seek the truth in love. Whichever side is wrong on such a fundamental issue cannot claim to have preserved the whole gospel; it cannot claim to be Christ's true Church. In true charity, neither side can let the other remain in error. True ecumenism means charitably *resolving* these kinds of doctrinal disagreements, not agreeing to disagree.

THREE WAYS JESUS IS PRESENT

But what's so special about Christ's presence in the Eucharist? Isn't Jesus present everywhere? To answer this common objection, we must distinguish three different ways Jesus can be present:

(1) Jesus is present everywhere *as God*, through His knowledge, power and essence. (This is called God's natural presence.)

(2) Jesus is present *spiritually* in those who are in the state of grace.

(3) Jesus is present in His *flesh and blood, soul and divinity*, in the Eucharist.

In His glorified human body, Jesus is present only in two places: at the right hand of the Father in heaven, and in the holy Eucharist on earth. As we shall see later, this flesh and blood presence provides us with a unique, life-giving power.

WHY SHOULD WE BELIEVE IN THE REAL PRESENCE?

The primary reason we should believe in the Real Presence is that the infallible teaching authority of the Catholic Church has proclaimed it for nearly 2000 years. Catholics believe, and historical evidence proves, the Catholic Church is the one true Church established by Jesus Christ to continue His work of teaching and sanctifying the world. Jesus appointed Apostles, with Peter as the head, to oversee His Church. He entrusted to them the fullness of the truth and the fullness of the means of salvation.[2]

Jesus gave the Apostles His own teaching authority (Luke 10:16). He promised to be with them until the end of time (Matthew 28:18–20). Finally, Jesus promised to send the Holy Spirit to guard the gospel perpetually (John 14:16, 26). The Apostles ordained successors, known as bishops, to carry on Christ's work of teaching, sanctifying, and governing. With the help of the Holy Spirit, this unbroken line of bishops has continued to use its Christ-given authority to guard, interpret, and proclaim the gospel of Jesus to the present day.

This apostolic Church gave us the Bible. The Church determined on its own authority which books were and were not inspired. As St. Augustine said, "I myself would not believe in the Gospel if the authority of the Catholic Church did not move me to do so."[3] This authoritative Church gives us the sacraments, the channels of grace. This same authoritative Church assures us that the doctrine of the Real Presence is true. If we accept the teaching authority of the Catholic Church, we must accept the Eucharist as she defines it.

Obviously, most non-Catholic Christians do not accept the teaching authority of the Catholic Church. Sadly, many Catholics reject it as well. However, we can still prove the Real Presence by appealing to the Bible[4] and to history. God has not only entrusted this truth to His Church, He has also revealed it in His Sacred Word, and confirmed it throughout history.

> *He who hears you hears me, and he who rejects you rejects me, and he who rejects me rejects him who sent me.*
>
> Luke 10:16

---

2 See our booklet, *Beginning Apologetics 1: How to Explain and Defend the Catholic Faith,* to prove that the Catholic Church is the one, true, apostolic Church established by Jesus.

3 *Against the Letter of Mani* 5, 6; William A. Jurgens, *The Faith of the Early Fathers* (Collegeville, MN: Liturgical Press, 1979) Volume 3, page 52, #1581.

4 Most Christians who reject the Catholic Church still accept the Bible as God's inspired word. They often don't realize that the Bible comes to them from the Catholic Church. In a series of councils at the end of the fourth century, the Catholic Church determined, *on her own authority*, which books are inspired and thus belong in the Bible. We should point out the inconsistency of *accepting* the Church's judgment about the contents of the Bible while *rejecting* the Church's authority to make that judgment. Undermining the authority of the Catholic Church logically undermines the credibility of the Bible. See our section on the "Canon of the Bible" in *Beginning Apologetics 1* to show how the Bible comes from the Church, not vice-versa.

THE BIBLICAL BASIS FOR THE REAL PRESENCE

The doctrine of Christ's Real Presence in the Eucharist is one of the easiest to demonstrate from Scripture. First, we'll examine how images of the Eucharist foreshadowed in the Old Testament are wonderfully realized in the New. Then, we'll see how Christ promises the Real Presence in John 6 and fulfills that promise at the Last Supper. Finally, we'll look at how the earliest Christians understood the Eucharist by examining 1 Corinthians, chapters 10 and 11.

THE EUCHARIST PREFIGURED IN THE OLD TESTAMENT

The Old Testament contains many signs and symbols of the Eucharist that are fulfilled in the New Testament:

(1) Melchizedek. The *bread and wine* offered by the priest-king Melchizedek (Genesis 14:18) prefigure the bread and wine offered by the eternal priest-king Jesus at the Last Supper. Remember that Hebrews 6:20 identifies Jesus as "high priest for ever after the order of Melchizedek."

(2) The Paschal Lamb. The same victim that was *offered up* to save the lives of the first-born of Israel was also the victim *consumed as food* for bodily nourishment as the Israelites began their journey to the promised land (Exodus 12:1–20). This prefigures the Eucharist where the same victim, Jesus, who was offered up for our sins to save us from spiritual death is consumed in the Eucharist to provide spiritual nourishment for the journey to our promised land of heaven.

(3) The Manna. This is one of the clearest symbols of the Eucharist in the Old Testament and one that Jesus expressly applies to Himself (John 6:32–51). The manna from heaven sustained the Israelites throughout their pilgrimage in the desert, but ceased to fall when they entered the Promised Land (Exodus 16:35). Similarly, the Eucharist nourishes us spiritually in this life of pilgrimage, but ceases (as do all the other sacraments) when we enter the promised land of heaven.

(4) The Ark of the Covenant. This holiest of containers in the Old Testament prefigures the tabernacles in our Catholic Churches because it contained three items, each of which prefigures the Eucharist:

(a) The *written word* of God on **tablets** (Exodus 25:16) which prefigures the *living word* contained in the Eucharist.

(b) A jar of **manna** (Exodus 16:34). This *ordinary bread* from heaven prefigures the Eucharist where Jesus—"*the living bread* which came down from heaven" (John 6:51)—comes to us under the appearance of bread.

(c) The **rod of Aaron** (Numbers 17:10 [RSV] or 17:25 in other Bibles) which flowered and bore *ripe almonds* as a sign of the *true priesthood* of the Old Covenant. Aaron's priesthood prefigures the high priesthood of Jesus Christ in the New Covenant. Aaron's rod, the sign of his priesthood, prefigures the instrument of Christ's priesthood, His body. By assuming a human nature, Jesus was able to offer up His flesh and blood as a perfect sacrifice for our sins. Just as Aaron's rod miraculously brought forth almonds, so Jesus' body miraculously brought forth the sacraments of baptism and the Eucharist, signified by the blood and water that flowed from His wounded side.

THE EUCHARIST FULFILLED IN THE NEW TESTAMENT

The Eucharist Promised in John 6

The clearest expression of the doctrine of the Real Presence is found in the sixth chapter of John's gospel. It is extremely important to remember that John 6 has two major, interconnected themes:

- Jesus' teaching about the *Eucharist*.
- Jesus' discussion about *faith*—the unique and special faith needed to accept His difficult teaching about the Holy Eucharist.

Indeed, as we read John 6, we will see how many of Jesus' own disciples lacked the faith required to believe in the Real Presence. When He walked the earth, it took great faith to believe Jesus was God since His humanity veiled His divinity. However, to believe that Jesus is present in the Eucharist requires even greater faith, because the Eucharist veils both His divinity and His humanity. This is why Jesus stresses the

> *John 6 has two major themes:* Faith *and the* Real Presence. *Obviously it takes a great deal of the first to accept the second.*

theme of faith so strongly at the same time He reveals His teaching on the Eucharist.

In this Eucharistic discourse (John 6:35–69), Jesus clearly teaches that we must consume His flesh and blood *as food*:

> "I am the living bread which came down from heaven; if any one eats of this bread, he will live for ever; and the bread which I shall give for the life of the world is my flesh" (verse 51). So Jesus said to them, "Truly, truly, I say to you, unless you eat the flesh of the Son of man and drink his blood, you have no life in you" (verse 53). "For my flesh is food indeed, and my blood is drink indeed" (verse 55).

It is no accident that immediately prior to the Eucharistic discourse, Jesus performs two of His most famous miracles, both of which emphasize faith:

- The multiplication of the loaves and the feeding of the 5000, wherein He tests Phillip's faith (John 6:6).
- The calming of the storm at sea, where Jesus reprimands Peter for his lack of faith (Matthew 14:31).

There are at least five reasons that we know Jesus was speaking *literally* and not symbolically about His real flesh and blood:

(1) This discourse takes place just after the famous miracle of the multiplication of the loaves. Jesus turned five loaves and a couple of fish into a seemingly inexhaustible food supply: enough to feed thousands of people and still fill twelve baskets with

leftovers! This miracle prefigures the inexhaustible gift of Christ's own flesh and blood, which is capable of being received by millions without being divided or diminished. Jesus claims that this miracle of ordinary bread is nothing compared to the miracle He will give us with the extraordinary bread of His own flesh.

(2) Jesus claims the *superiority* of His bread over the manna given to the Israelites. "I am the bread of life. Your fathers ate the manna in the wilderness, and they died. This is the bread which comes down from heaven that a man may eat of it and not die" (verses 48–50). The miracle of the manna was enormous: every day several million Israelites received an omer (about two quarts) of manna per person. This amounts to several hundred tons of manna raining down daily (except for the Sabbath) for forty years! Jesus says that He will perform an even greater miracle than the manna. But mere earthly, natural bread serving as a symbol of Christ would be *inferior* to the heavenly, supernatural manna. The bread Christ gives us must be *more real* and *more miraculous* than even the manna.

(3) Everyone who heard Jesus understood Him to be speaking *literally* of His own body and blood. "How can this man give us his flesh to eat?" object the unbelieving Jews (verse 52). "This is a hard saying; who can listen to it?" demand His unbelieving disciples (verse 60). Many of these disciples had lived, eaten, and walked with Jesus for nearly two

> *"For my flesh is* food indeed, *and my blood is* drink indeed" (*John 6:55*). *This is not the language of symbolism!*

years. They spoke the same language and dialect as Jesus. Day in and day out, they heard Him use different figures of speech. They heard Him speak symbolically, using parables, allegories, and analogies (such as calling Herod a fox). They also heard Him speak literally, meaning exactly what He said. In Christ's Eucharistic discourse, these disciples heard Him "live." If a picture is worth a thousand words, then a live presentation is worth a thousand pictures. Yet these same disciples—many of whom quit following Christ—never even asked Jesus to explain Himself. They understood perfectly that Jesus meant precisely what He said![5]

(4) Instead of explaining that His listeners were misunderstanding Him, that He was only speaking figuratively, Jesus—using the strongest possible language—emphatically *repeats* the literalness of this teaching, six times in six verses (verses 53–58)! "Truly, truly, I say to you, unless you eat the flesh of the Son of man and drink his blood, you have no life in you" (verse 53). "For my flesh is *food indeed*, and my blood is *drink indeed*" (verse 55). This is *not* the language of symbolism!

---

5 The entire audience who heard and saw Jesus firsthand testified by their reactions that He was speaking literally. How can we—reading a translation of ancient languages nearly 2000 years later—reasonably maintain that Jesus was only speaking symbolically? We simply can't. It would be the height of arrogance to assume that all the eye- and ear-witnesses got it wrong, while we—far removed in time, place, language, and culture—got it right!

12

When people *wrongly* take Him literally, Jesus *corrects* and *explains*:	When people *rightly* take Him literally, Jesus *confirms* and *repeats*:
Jesus answered him, "Truly, truly, I say to you, unless one is born anew, he cannot see the kingdom of God." Nicodemus said to him, "How can a man be born when he is old? Can he enter a second time into his mother's womb and be born?" Jesus answered, "Truly, truly, I say to you, unless one is born of water and the Spirit, he cannot enter the kingdom of God" (John 3:3–5).	When Jesus saw their faith he said to the paralytic, "Take heart, my son; your sins are forgiven." And behold, some of the scribes said to themselves, "This man is blaspheming." But Jesus, knowing their thoughts, said, "Why do you think evil in your hearts? For which is easier, to say, 'Your sins are forgiven' or to say, 'Rise and walk'? But that you may know that the Son of Man has authority on earth to forgive sins"—he then said to the paralytic—"Rise, take up your bed and go home" (Matthew 9:2–6).
Thus he spoke, and then said to them, "Our friend Lazarus has fallen asleep, but I go to awake him out of sleep." The disciples said to him, "Lord, if he has fallen asleep, he will recover." Now Jesus had spoken of His death, but they thought he meant taking rest in sleep. Then Jesus told them plainly, "Lazarus is dead" (John 11:11–14).	"Your father Abraham rejoiced that he was able to see my day; he saw it and was glad." The Jews then said to him, "You are not yet fifty years old, and have you seen Abraham?" Jesus said to them, "Truly, truly, I say to you, before Abraham was, I am." So they took up stones to throw at him; but Jesus hid himself, and went out of the temple (John 8:56–59).
"Again I tell you, it is easier for a camel to go through the eye of a needle than for a rich man to enter the kingdom of God." When the disciples heard this they were greatly astonished, saying, "Who then can be saved?" But Jesus looked at them and said to them, "With men this is impossible, but with God all things are possible" (Matthew 19:24–26).	They said, "Is not this Jesus, the son of Joseph, whose father and mother we know? How does he now say, 'I have come down from heaven'?" Jesus answered them, "Do not murmur among yourselves.... Every one who has heard and learned from the Father comes to me. Not that any one has seen the Father except him who is from God; he has seen the Father.... This is the bread which comes down from heaven, that a man may eat of it and not die. I am the living bread which came down from heaven" (John 6:41–51).[6]
Again he said to them, "I go away, and you will seek me and die in your sin; where I am going, you cannot come." Then said the Jews, "Will he kill himself, since he says, 'Where I am going, you cannot come'?" He said to them, "You are from below, I am from above; you are of this world, I am not of this world" (John 8:21–23).	
Jesus said to the Jews who had believed in him, "...you will know the truth, and the truth will set you free." They answered him, "We are descendants of Abraham, and have never been in bondage to any one. How is it that you say, 'You will be made free'?" Jesus answered them, "Truly, truly, I say to you, every one who commits sin is a slave to sin.... So if the Son makes you free, you will be free indeed" (John 8:31–36).	
Jesus then said to them, "Truly, truly, I say to you, it was not Moses who gave you the bread from heaven; my Father gives you the true bread from heaven. For the bread of God is that which comes down from heaven, and gives life to the world." They said to him, "Lord, give us this bread always." Jesus said to them, "I am the bread of life; he who comes to me shall not hunger, and he who believes in me shall never thirst" (John 6:32–35).	

When the Jews object to Jesus saying that the bread He will give is His flesh, does Jesus explain Himself or repeat Himself? Jesus emphatically *repeats* Himself, six times in a row, confirming that He intends to be understood literally.

(5) Many of Jesus' own disciples can't accept the literalness of His teaching and leave Him (verse 66). Notice that Jesus *doesn't* call

6 We are indebted to Nicholas Cardinal Wiseman's *The Real Presence of the Body and Blood of our Lord Jesus in the Blessed Eucharist* (London, England: Burns Oates & Washbourne, 1942) for this and many other insights.

them back and explain that He is only speaking figuratively, as He did on previous occasions when they mistook His words literally. For example, in John 4:31–34, Jesus says, "I have food to eat of which you do not know." His disciples take Him literally, so Jesus explains: "My food is to do the will of Him who sent me…." In Matthew 16:5–12, Jesus says, "Beware of the leaven of the Pharisees and Sadducees." Once again, His disciples think Jesus is speaking literally. Again, Jesus corrects them and explains that He is not talking about real bread. "Then they understood that he did not tell them to beware of the leaven of bread, but the teaching of the Pharisees and Sadducees."

Jesus *doesn't* call the unbelieving disciples back and offer to explain for an obvious reason: they understood exactly what He meant! They just couldn't accept it. Even the twelve Apostles are shaken. But Jesus doesn't compromise one bit. Instead, He challenges His own handpicked Apostles: "Will you also go away?" (verse 67). In faith Peter answers: "Lord, to whom shall we go? You have the words of eternal life" (verse 69). We have two choices: we can either doubt like the unbelieving Jews and disciples, or believe like Peter that somehow Christ will accomplish His promise. Notice that Judas apparently rejects this teaching (verse 70–71).

Reading carefully, we can see why Jesus stresses the theme of faith so strongly (especially in verses 61–65). The Jewish multitudes and many of His own disciples reject Christ's teaching because of their lack of faith. We Catholics should appreciate and nurture this special gift of faith that enables us to believe in the Real Presence. We should pray for our non-Catholic brothers and sisters who aren't able to accept this glorious mystery that is so far beyond our understanding.

Answering Objections

(1) *Isn't Jesus only speaking figuratively when He says we must eat His body and drink His blood?*

Answer: No. Jesus couldn't be speaking figuratively, because that expression already had a *specific figurative meaning*. In the Aramaic language of our Lord, to figuratively "eat the flesh" or "drink the blood" of someone meant to persecute, assault, and destroy him. This Hebrew expression is found in many scripture passages (see table below).

Verses showing "eating flesh" and "drinking blood" as a figure of speech for assault and persecution	
Psalm 27:2	When evildoers come at me to devour my flesh (*NAB*).
Isaiah 9:18–20	they devour on the left, but are not satisfied; each devours his neighbour's flesh.
Isaiah 49:26	I will make your oppressors eat their own flesh, and they shall be drunk with their own blood as with wine.
Micah 3:3	who eat the flesh of my people…and chop them up like meat in a kettle, like flesh in a cauldron.
2 Samuel 23:15–17	"Shall I drink the blood of the men who went at the risk of their lives?" Therefore [David] would not drink it.
Revelation 17:6, 16	they will make her desolate and naked, and devour her flesh and burn her up with fire.

If Jesus is speaking only *figuratively* about eating His flesh and drinking His blood, as non-Catholics claim, then what He really means is "*whoever persecutes, assaults, and destroys me will have eternal life.*" This makes nonsense of the passage!

14

(2) *Look at John 6:35: "I am the bread of life; he who comes to me shall not hunger, and he who believes in me shall never thirst." When Jesus calls Himself the "bread of life" isn't He simply saying that if we believe in Him, He will nourish us spiritually, just as bread nourishes us physically? Don't we "eat" and "drink" Jesus, our spiritual food, by coming to and believing in Him?*

Answer: Yes, of course. If Jesus had said no more than that, Catholics wouldn't believe in the Real Presence. But Jesus doesn't stop at verse 35. Remember, the "bread of life" discourse has two parts. In the first (verses 22–47), Jesus primarily stresses the necessity of *believing* in Him. In the second (verses 48–59), Jesus goes on to tell us exactly what He means by calling Himself "bread."

The bread Jesus is speaking of is not merely a symbol for spiritual nourishment. Jesus tells us plainly that *the bread is His own flesh, the very same flesh that He is going to offer for the life of the world* (verse 51). Think about this. Jesus *equates* the flesh we must eat for eternal life with the flesh offered on the cross! Either they are both literal or they are both figurative. No Christian doubts that Christ offered His *real* flesh on the cross. Therefore, we cannot doubt that Christ wants us to eat His *real* flesh for our salvation.

When Jesus explains that the bread of life is literally His flesh, we must accept His clear words. We cannot prefer a different explanation to the one Jesus Himself provides. Believing in Jesus (the teaching of the first part of the discourse) means also believing that He will give us His actual flesh and blood to eat (the teaching of the second part).

(3) *In John 6:60–70, doesn't Jesus explain He was only speaking symbolically in the previous verses? Notice verse 63: "It is the spirit that gives life, the flesh is of no avail; the words that I have spoken to you are spirit and life."*

Answer: No, verse 63 doesn't prove Jesus was speaking symbolically about the Eucharist for the following reasons:

(1) Jesus' Eucharistic discourse *ends* with verse 58 (see verse 59). The dialogue of verses 60–70 occurs *later* and deals with *faith*, not the Eucharist.

(2) The word "spirit" is nowhere used in the Bible to mean "symbolic." The spiritual is every bit as real as the material.

(3) In verse 63, Jesus is contrasting the natural or carnal man ("the flesh") with the spiritual or faith-filled man. 1 Corinthians 2:14–3:4 offers a good explanation of what Jesus means by "the flesh":

> The unspiritual man does not receive the gifts of the Spirit of God, for they are folly to him, and he is not able to understand them because they are spiritually discerned. The spiritual man judges all things, but is himself to be judged by no one. "For who has known the mind of the Lord so as to instruct him?" But we have the mind of Christ. But I, brethren, could not address you as spiritual men, but as men of the flesh, as babes in Christ. I fed you with milk, not solid food; for you were not ready for it; and even yet you are not ready, for you are still of the flesh. For while there is jealousy and strife among you, are you not of *the flesh, and behaving like ordinary men*? For when one says, "I belong to Paul," and another, "I belong to Apollos," are you not merely men?

The contrast between the flesh (human thoughts and desires) and the spirit (human thoughts and desires elevated by grace) is made in Romans 8:1–13, especially verses 5–9:

> For those who live according to the flesh set their minds on the things of the flesh, but those who live according to the Spirit set their minds on the things of the Spirit. To set the mind on the flesh is death, but to set the mind on the Spirit is life and peace. For the mind that is set on the flesh is hostile to God; it does not submit to God's law, indeed it cannot; and those who are in the flesh cannot please God. But you are not in the flesh, you are in the Spirit, if the Spirit of God really dwells in you. Any one who does not have the Spirit of Christ does not belong to him.

Verses confirming that "the flesh" refers to natural thoughts and desires while "the spirit" refers to supernatural thoughts and desires:[7]	
Matthew 26:41	The spirit indeed is willing, but the flesh is weak.
John 3:6	That which is born of the flesh is flesh, and that which is born of the Spirit is spirit.
Galatians 5:13–26	walk by the Spirit, and do not gratify the desires of the flesh. For the desires of the flesh are against the Spirit, and the desires of the Spirit are against the flesh....
Romans 7:5–6, 25	While we were living in the flesh, our sinful passions, aroused by the law, were at work in our members to bear fruit for death.
Galatians 3:3, 4:29	Are you so foolish? Having begun with the Spirit, are you now ending with the flesh? ... But as at that time he who was born according to the flesh persecuted him who was born according to the Spirit, so it is now.
Romans 13:14	But put on the Lord Jesus Christ, and make no provision for the flesh, to gratify its desires.

7 Also see 1 John 2:16; Galatians 6:8; 1 Peter 2:11.

(4) Notice that Jesus says "*my* flesh" when discussing the Eucharist. He says "*the* flesh" when referring to the carnal man who will not believe anything beyond his senses and reason. No Christian believes that *Jesus'* flesh is "of no avail," for His flesh was the means of our redemption.

(5) The unbelieving disciples leave Jesus *after* verse 63. *They would not have left at this point if Jesus had assured them that He was only speaking symbolically.* This is the only time in the New Testament that any of Jesus' disciples abandon Him because they find a doctrine of His too hard to accept.

The Promise Fulfilled at the Last Supper

Jesus fulfills His promise to give His literal flesh and blood as food and drink at the Last Supper. The New Testament records the Last Supper four times: Matthew 26:26–30, Mark 14:22–26, Luke 22:14–20, and 1 Corinthians 11:23–26. At the all-powerful words of Christ, "This *is* my body ... This *is* my blood," the bread and the wine are completely changed into Christ's actual flesh and blood.

To believe in the Real Presence is simply to take Jesus at His word. If He declares ordinary bread and wine to be His true flesh and blood then, by the all-powerful word of God, that's what they become! God created light by merely saying, "Let there be light." Jesus cured the royal official's son in Capernaum by merely *affirming* that he was healed (John 4:46–53). Jesus took every opportunity to convince the Apostles of His omnipotence: He had cured every kind of disease and infirmity, raised people from the dead, changed water into wine, calmed the storm, walked on water, and multiplied a few loaves to satisfy a huge crowd. He had done everything to prepare the Apostles to accept the truth of His declarations, no matter how extraordinary they sounded.

Just as He did in John 6, Jesus **equates** His body and blood given in the Eucharist with His body and blood sacrificed on the cross. "This is my body, *which is given for* you" (Luke 22:19); "this is my blood of the covenant, *which is poured out* for many for the forgiveness of sins" (Matthew 26:28). Jesus identifies the body and blood He gives at the Last Supper as the **very same** body and blood that He will sacrifice on Calvary. If we accept the body and blood offered on the cross as literal (as all Christians do), then we must also accept the body and blood offered in the Eucharist as literal.

If Christ isn't speaking literally, why does He use such clear and simple words on such a solemn occasion, the night before His suffering and death on the cross? At the Last Supper, on the eve of His passion, Jesus gives His "last will and testament." This was definitely a time for plain and literal speech (see Mark 4:34).

The Eucharist was celebrated on Passover, and so the Eucharist is the fulfillment of the Jewish Passover sacrifice. This ritual required that the paschal lamb be *eaten* (Exodus 12:8, 46) to avoid the death of the first-born. John the Baptist calls Jesus the "Lamb of God" (John 1:29) and St. Paul calls Christ "our paschal lamb," who "has been sacrificed" (1 Corinthians 5:7). We must eat the flesh of our paschal lamb, Jesus the Lamb of God, who takes away the sins of the world. Israelites who didn't eat the paschal lamb didn't share in the benefits of the lamb's sacrifice (freedom from bodily death). Similarly, if we don't consume the true Paschal Lamb in the Eucharist, we won't share in the merits of the Lamb's sacrifice on Calvary (freedom from spiritual death).

Answering Objections

(1) Jesus calls Himself a "vine" (John 15:1) and a "door" (John 10:9). But He isn't literally a vine or a door. Can't we suppose that Jesus is likewise speaking figuratively when He says, "This is my body; this is my blood"?

Answer: No. When Jesus calls Himself the vine or the door, the context clearly shows that He is speaking figuratively. John 10:6 expressly calls the illustration of the door a "figure of speech." Furthermore, these figures of speech or analogies are very straight-forward: Jesus is *like* a vine that gives spiritual life to all Christians, the branches. Jesus is *like* a door through which all men must come who seek salvation. There is an obvious comparison between Jesus and the vine or door. But what on earth could Jesus mean by holding up a piece of bread and saying, "This is like my body"? We can see how Jesus is like a vine or a door, but how is His body like bread? How is His blood like wine? There is no obvious comparison between His body and bread or between His blood and wine.

In contrast, everything about the Last Supper suggests that Jesus is speaking literally: His repeated promises in John 6 that His flesh and blood are true food and drink; the solemnity of the occasion, the straightforward speech, and the total lack of a figurative comparison between the bread and wine and Jesus' body and blood. Furthermore, He equates the body and blood given at the Last Supper with the body and blood given on Calvary.

Finally, there is a difference in grammar. "I am the vine" cannot be literally true, for a man can never literally be a plant. It's a contradiction to say that two materials things can literally be the same thing. At the Last Supper, Jesus did not say, "*Bread* is my body" (which would be a contradiction). Instead He said, "*This* is my body." The "this" in this statement remains unspecified until it is identified as the body of Christ. So there is no contradiction in taking this statement literally, as there would be if we took literally the statements about the vine and door.

(2) If the Apostles consumed Jesus' real body and blood, wouldn't they be committing cannibalism? Furthermore, wouldn't this violate the biblical prohibition against drinking blood?

Answer: No. It was precisely this mis-understanding that led the unbelieving Jews and disciples in John 6 to reject Jesus when He said they must eat His body and drink His blood. They thought Jesus was commanding them to consume Him in a bloody, cannibalistic way. However, the believing disciples were rewarded for their faith at the Last Supper. Jesus revealed that they would receive His true body and blood *sacramentally* (present in a hidden way).

> *While the Apostles truly consumed Christ's real body and blood, it wasn't cannibalism, because Christ wasn't in His natural condition.*

In the sacrament of the Eucharist, Christ's body and blood are truly present, but not with their normal physical properties. Jesus' body isn't spread out in space; its normal condition is hidden under the appearance of bread and wine. While the Apostles truly consumed Christ's real body and blood, it wasn't cannibalism, because Christ wasn't in His natural condition. They didn't bite off pieces of Christ's arm, for example, or swallow quantities of His blood; instead they received Christ whole and entire—body, blood, soul, and divinity—under the appearance of bread and wine. Receiving Christ's real, but sacramental presence in the Eucharist has nothing to do with cannibalism or drinking blood.

(3) How could Jesus give His body and blood to His disciples and still be there in the room? Isn't it impossible for Jesus' body and blood to be in two places at once?

Answer: Mysterious, yes, but not impossible. Christ was present at the Last Supper in two ways: (1) at the table with His disciples in a *natural* way; and (2) under the appearance of bread and wine in a *sacramental* way. Just because we can't understand *how* God does something is no reason to doubt *that* He does it. Many Christian beliefs are beyond our comprehension: How can there be three, distinct Persons in only one God? How can Jesus be both fully God and fully man? How can God create everything out of nothing? How can God be present everywhere in the universe at the same time?

Yet all Christians accept the mysteries of the Trinity, the Incarnation, creation, and God's omnipresence. That's what a mystery means: a revealed truth that cannot be *completely* understood. If we can accept the overwhelming mystery of Christ's divinity, we should have no trouble accepting His teachings, however difficult they may seem.

Obviously nothing is impossible for God (Luke 1:37). But Jesus prepared us to accept the idea of something being in different places simultaneously. Recall the miracle of the loaves and fishes, where a limited amount of food was miraculously multiplied to feed thousands of people at the same time. If Jesus could multiply the presence of natural bread, we should have no trouble believing that He could multiply the presence of His body.

The Witness of St. Paul

The Apostles continued to celebrate the Eucharist in obedience to Christ's command, "do this in memory of me." Did the early Christians believe in the literal flesh and blood presence of Christ in the Eucharist? Did the Apostles believe that they:

> *Paul's words in 1 Corinthians 10 and 11 are meaningless without the Real Presence.*

(a) distributed mere bread and wine as a symbol or memory of Christ; or

(b) consecrated the actual body and blood of Christ?

Consider the witness of St. Paul in his first letter to the Corinthians: "The cup of blessing which we bless, is it not a participation in the blood of Christ? The bread which we break, is it not a participation in the body of Christ?"

(1 Corinthians 10:16). St. Paul says that in the Eucharist we participate in Christ's own body and blood, not in a mere symbol or memory of Christ. Symbolic bread and wine cannot unite us to Christ's real body and blood. The only way to *participate* in Jesus' body and blood through the Eucharist is if His body and blood are *really present* in the Eucharist.

St. Paul warns Christians not to receive the Eucharist unworthily:

> Whoever, therefore, eats the bread or drinks the cup of the Lord in an unworthy manner will be *guilty of profaning the body and blood of the Lord* (1 Corinthians 11:27).

In St. Paul's time, the expression "to answer for the body and blood" of someone meant to be guilty of murder, of shedding that person's blood. If we receive the Eucharist in an unworthy manner, we are guilty of a sacrilege comparable to shedding Christ's blood. We cannot be guilty of murder if we only violate someone's symbolic presence. For example, if a man beheads a statue of the pope or stomps on a picture of his wife, he might be guilty of disrespect, but certainly not assault, much less murder. Damaging a symbol doesn't damage the person. How can we be held to "answer for the body and blood of the Lord" if His body and blood aren't really there in the Eucharist? Paul's words are meaningless without the Real Presence.

St. Paul continues:

> Let a man examine himself, and so eat of the bread and drink of the cup. For any one

who eats and drinks *without discerning the body* eats and drinks *judgment* [damnation] upon himself (1 Corinthians 11:28–29).

St. Paul says we are condemned for not recognizing and acknowledging the body of the Lord. How can we be held accountable for not discerning the body of the Lord in the Eucharist if it is only a bit of bread and wine? The possibility of *not recognizing* Jesus in the Eucharist implies that He is actually there to recognize. Do you discern the body of Christ in the Eucharist? That is the question we must ask ourselves and our non-Catholic brothers and sisters.

Answering Objections

Even after consecration, Jesus calls the contents of the cup, "the fruit of the vine" (Matthew 26:29) and St. Paul continues to call the other element "bread" (1 Corinthians 11:26, 27, 28). Doesn't this prove that they are still bread and wine?

Answer: No. Scripture often calls things by their appearance. Angels who appear as men are called men (Genesis 18:2, 22; 19:1). The Holy Spirit is described as "tongues of fire" descending upon the Apostles (Acts 2:3).

Scripture also calls things by their former names. For example, after Aaron's rod was turned into a serpent, it is still called a rod: "But Aaron's rod swallowed up their rods" (Exodus 7:12). After Jesus cured the man born blind, he is still called "the blind man" (John 9:17).

No one would argue that the angels weren't really angels because they are called men. No one would argue that the man born blind wasn't really cured because he is later referred to as the blind man. Likewise, we can't argue that the Eucharist isn't the body and blood of Christ just because it is sometimes called bread and wine. The Eucharist is called bread after consecration because it retains the *appearance* of bread, and because it was bread *before* its consecration.

A Final Observation Concerning the Scriptural Proofs

We have examined more than a dozen passages concerning the Eucharist. Every one of them affirms, in the strongest possible language, the doctrine of the Real Presence of Christ in the Eucharist. On the other hand, not a single passage in all of Scripture affirms or even suggests the real absence. We have no choice but to accept the clear, forceful, and repeated declarations of God's Word.

Protestants claim to follow the plain sense of Scripture as their only rule. How then can they deny so many clear assertions of the Bible, especially when not a single verse authorizes them to do so? Jesus says, "the bread that I will give is my flesh for the life of the world" (John 6:51); yet Protestants maintain, "it is not His flesh, but only a bit of bread." Christ says, "This is my body" (Mt 26:26), but Protestants claim, "It is not His body." Whom should we believe?

> Christ says,
> "This is my body"
> (Mt 26:26),
> but Protestants claim,
> "It is not His body."
> Whom should we believe?

THE HISTORICAL BASIS FOR THE REAL PRESENCE

EVIDENCE FROM THE EARLY CHURCH FATHERS

The early Church Fathers are an irreplaceable link to early Christianity. Not only are they indispensable witnesses for the teachings of the apostolic Church, but they are also indispensable witnesses for the authorship and authenticity of the Scriptures. They testified that the Apostles preached what they preached, and wrote what they wrote. Some were eyewitnesses to the lives and teachings of the Apostles. They guarded and passed on these apostolic teachings from one generation to the next.

> *"The Christianity of history is not Protestantism.... To be deep in history is to cease to be a Protestant."*

Without the witness of those who knew the Apostles firsthand and who preserved and guaranteed their teachings, we wouldn't have a Bible. We wouldn't know that Matthew wrote Matthew or that John wrote John, since their names aren't included in the text. We wouldn't know that St. Paul really existed and actually wrote the letters ascribed to him. Ignoring or denying the testimony of the early Church Fathers destroys the credibility of the Bible itself. It is only through these faithful witnesses to the Apostles that we have received the Gospel.[8] The early Church Fathers are our only bridge to Christ and His Apostles. That bridge is unmistakably, undeniably Catholic.

Virtually every distinctively Catholic doctrine is clearly found in the writings of the early Fathers of the 1st, 2nd, 3rd, and 4th centuries. This includes the Real Presence of Christ in the Eucharist, the Mass as a sacrifice, apostolic succession, the primacy of Peter, intercessory prayer to the saints, devotion to Mary, purgatory, and confession to a priest. Many Fundamentalists like to think they have returned to "primitive Christianity." However, the evidence of the early Church Fathers proves that primitive Christians were unmistakeably *Catholics.*

John Henry Cardinal Newman, in his famous survey of Church history, *Essay on the Development of Christian Doctrine*, puts it bluntly:

> The Christianity of history is not Protestantism. If ever there were a safe truth, it is this. And Protestantism has ever felt it so.... This is shown in the determination ... of dispensing with historical Christianity altogether, and of forming a Christianity from the Bible alone: men never would have put it aside, unless they had despaired of it.... *To be deep in history is to cease to be a Protestant.*[9]

---

[8] The early Church Fathers preserved both the *written* and *oral* teachings of the Apostles. If they can't be trusted to have preserved their oral teachings, then they can't be trusted to have preserved their written teachings. On the other hand, if we accept their testimony about the New Testament, then we must also accept their testimony about apostolic tradition and the beliefs of the early Church.

[9] *Essay on the Development of Christian Doctrine* (Notre Dame, IN: Notre Dame Press, 1989), 7–8.

St. Ignatius of Antioch was a disciple and co-worker of the Apostle John.[10] He was the third bishop of Antioch, an important center of Christianity in the apostolic period. Around AD 110, St. Ignatius wrote seven letters to various churches on his way to be martyred in Rome. In his letter to the Smyrnaeans, St. Ignatius describes those who reject the Real Presence of Christ in the Eucharist as heretics:

> Take note of those who hold heterodox opinions on the grace of Jesus Christ which has come to us, and see how contrary their opinions are to the mind of God.... They abstain from the Eucharist and from prayer, because *they do not confess that the Eucharist is the Flesh of our Savior Jesus Christ*, Flesh which suffered for our sins and which the Father, in His goodness, raised up again.[11]

In his letter to the Romans, St. Ignatius writes:

> I have no taste for corruptible food nor for the pleasures of this life. I desire the Bread of God, which is the *Flesh* of Jesus Christ, who was of the seed of David; and for drink I desire His *Blood*, which is love incorruptible.[12]

St. Justin Martyr was born about the time the last Apostle, St. John, died in Ephesus. Justin converted in Ephesus around AD 130, where he was undoubtedly instructed by disciples of St. John undoubtedly instructed

him. He is considered the greatest Christian apologist of the second century. Around AD 150, in his famous *Apology* to the Emperor at Rome, St. Justin writes:

> We call this food Eucharist; and no one is permitted to partake of it, except one who believes our teaching to be true.... For *not as common bread nor common drink do we receive these*; but since Jesus Christ our Savior was made incarnate by the word of God and had both flesh and blood for our salvation, so too, as we have been taught, the food which has been made into *the Eucharist* by the Eucharistic prayer set down by Him, and by the change of which our blood and flesh is nourished, *is both the Flesh and the Blood of that incarnated Jesus*.[13]

St. Irenaeus is another very important early Father. He was bishop of Lyons and lived from AD 140–202. St. Irenaeus studied under St. Polycarp, who was a disciple of St. John the Apostle. St. Irenaeus is considered the greatest theologian of the immediate post-apostolic period. His masterpiece *Against Heresies* completely demolished the heretical views that threatened the post-apostolic Church. Around AD 195, St. Irenaeus writes:

> He [Jesus] has declared the cup, a part of creation, to be *His own Blood*, from which He causes our blood to flow; and the bread, a part of creation, He has established as *His own Body*, from which He gives increase to our bodies.[14]

St. Cyril of Jerusalem, in a catechetical lecture given in AD 350, says:

> He [Jesus] himself, therefore, having declared and said of the Bread, "This is My

---

[10] As an intimate disciple of the author of John 6, St. Ignatius is in a unique position to tell us whether Jesus was speaking literally or figuratively about the need to eat His flesh and drink His blood.

[11] *Letter to Smyrnaeans* 6, 2; Jurgens, #64.

[12] *Letter to the Romans* 7, 3; Jurgens, #54a.

[13] *First Apology* 66, 20; Jurgens, #128.

[14] *Against Heresies* 5, 2, 2; Jurgens, #249.

22

Body," who will dare any longer to doubt? And when He Himself has affirmed and said, "This is My Blood," who can ever hesitate and say it is not His Blood?[15]

Do not, therefore, regard the bread and wine as simply that, *for they are*, according to the Master's declaration, *the Body and Blood of Christ*. Even though the senses suggest to you the other, let faith make you firm. Do not judge in this matter by taste, but be fully assured by faith, not doubting that you have been deemed worthy of the *Body and Blood of Christ*.[16]

These early Fathers prove that early Christians firmly believed in the Real Presence of Christ in the Eucharist.[17] Notice that St. Ignatius was personally instructed by St. John the Apostle. St. Justin Martyr and St. Irenaeus each had direct contact with St. John's disciples. These three men are first- and second-generation disciples of the author of John 6! Who could be in a better position to tell us whether Jesus was speaking literally or figuratively about the need to eat His body and drink His blood? No one. These witnesses are as close as we can get to the apostolic Church. Their testimony is irrefutable and unmistakable: the Christian Church believed in the Real Presence from the very beginning.

EVIDENCE FROM HISTORY

Virtually all Christians accepted the doctrine of the Real Presence until the Reformation. All the Churches that broke away from the Catholic Church *before* the Reformation still believe in the Real Presence of Christ in the Eucharist. The Nestorians and Eutychians (who separated from the Catholic Church in the 5th century), as well as the Coptic (5th century), Armenian (5th century), and Orthodox (11th century) Churches—none of which has been in communion with Rome since then—still believe in the Real Presence. This demonstrates that the doctrine was part of the Christian deposit of faith at least as far back as the 5th century, before these splits occurred.

Suppose for a moment that the Catholic doctrine of the Real Presence is false. Jesus must have foreseen that the whole Church would embrace this false doctrine and fall into idolatry. He would have known that the very words He spoke in John 6 and at the Last Supper led them to do so. Why would He have deliberately used language that He knew Christians would misinterpret? Why would Jesus have allowed His followers to be so

---

15 *Catechetical Lectures*: 22 (*Mystagogic* 4), 1; Jurgens, #843.

16 *Catechetical Lectures*: 22 (*Mystagogic* 4), 6; Jurgens, #846.

17 Martin Luther himself confirms that the early Church Fathers unanimously taught the Real Presence: "of all the fathers, as many as you can name, not one has ever spoken about the sacrament as these fanatics do. None of them uses such an expression as, 'It is simply bread and wine,' or 'Christ's body and blood are not present.' Yet this subject is so frequently discussed by them, it is impossible that they should not at some time have let slip such an expression as, 'It is simply bread,' or 'Not that the body of Christ is physically present,' or the like, since they are greatly concerned not to mislead the people; actually, they simply proceed to speak as if no one doubted that Christ's body and blood are present. Certainly among so many fathers and so many writings a negative argument should have turned up at least once, as happens in other articles; but actually they all stand uniformly and consistently on the affirmative side" (*Luther's Works*, St. Louis, MI: Concordia Publishing, 1961, Volume 37, 54).

horribly mistaken when He could have prevented it with a simple word of explanation? It is simply impossible that the Divine Teacher was so clumsy in proclaiming His doctrines that He led all His students into error.

Suppose again that Jesus intended to be understood figuratively and that the Apostles taught a *symbolic* understanding of the Eucharist. How then can we explain the development of the doctrine of the Real Presence? If Christians first believed in the symbolic presence, then the doctrine of the Real Presence must have appeared as *novel* and unheard of. It must have been considered *false* and *heretical*, because it was diametrically opposed to what all Christians are supposed to have believed as a revealed truth. It must have even appeared a most dangerous heresy, because it teaches *idolatry*: adoring mere bread and wine as God Himself. Finally, it must have appeared altogether *incredible*: contrary to the senses, to reason, and to faith.

Human nature doesn't change. The same reasons that make the Real Presence appear unbelievable today would have made it appear unbelievable then. The same objections people raise today—it looks and tastes like ordinary bread and wine, it seems impossible for God to be present under the appearances of bread and wine—people would have raised then. With all these disadvantages, such a novel doctrine could never have been embraced by even a small number of reasonable people, much less

the whole Church. Christians could never have believed this doctrine unless they thought it was revealed by God Himself, whose divine authority removes all difficulties. This belief could never have taken root in the Church if Jesus Himself hadn't revealed it and delivered it to the Apostles.

Remember that those who reject the Real Presence of Christ in the Eucharist are departing from the clear evidence in Scripture and from 1500 years of virtually unanimous[18] Christian teaching. By rights, it's not Catholics who should defend themselves for *holding fast* to this doctrine, but rather non-Catholics who should defend themselves for *departing* from it. Non-Catholics must justify why they prefer the recent inventions of the Reformers to the ancient and unbroken teaching of Christ's apostolic Church.

EVIDENCE FROM EUCHARISTIC MIRACLES

Through the centuries, God has performed miracles to confirm His Real Presence in the Eucharist. From the beginning, Christians have reported astounding events surrounding the Eucharist: including hosts that levitated, bled, or became hard as stone when received by a person in mortal sin; and people who lived for years on the Eucharist alone.

---

18 The first Christian to challenge the Real Presence is Berengarius of Tours (about 1010–1088), who later retracted his views. In the 12th and 13th centuries, a few heretical groups denied the Real Presence (Cathari or Albigensians). In the 14th century, John Wycliff (1330–1384) resurrected Berengarius' objections and tried to present them as the views of the early Church. Wycliff's ideas influenced subsequent 16th-century Protestant Reformers such as Ulrich Zwingli and John Calvin.

There are many well-documented Eucharistic miracles, but we will examine only two.[19] The first occurred in Lanciano, Italy in the 8th century. The second involved a 20th-century woman whose sole food for 40 years was the Eucharist.

Around AD 700, a priest in a monastery in Lanciano had serious doubts about the Real Presence of Christ in the Eucharist. One morning at Mass, as he finished saying the words of consecration, the host suddenly turned into a circle of flesh and the wine became visible blood. The astonished priest realized that God had just dramatically answered his doubts. The people in the Church were amazed, and soon the whole town buzzed with the news of a miracle. The host and blood were put on permanent display in the church.

This miracle has been examined through the centuries, without any trace of fakery. Pope Paul VI encouraged a scientific investigation in 1971, by Italian doctors using sophisticated equipment. They concluded that the flesh is real human flesh and the blood is real human blood. The flesh is from a human heart, expertly dissected. The blood is type AB, and has all the normal proteins found in fresh human blood. Even though the flesh and blood have been exposed to the air for 1200 years, they are biologically undamaged.

Many people have lived on nothing but the Eucharist for varying lengths of time. St. Catherine of Siena, St. Joseph of Cupertino, and St. Rose of Lima are some of the better-known saints who have lived on Holy Communion alone.

A German lay woman, Therese Neumann (1898–1962), lived the last 36 years of her life without any food or water other than Holy Communion. In 1922, at the age of 24, Therese's body rejected any food but the Eucharist. At the direction of her spiritual advisor, she did have a sip of water to help her digest the host. By 1926, even the water proved unnecessary.

Receiving Holy Communion gave her a surge of energy, allowing her to engage in vigorous farm and house work. She required no sleep, often going to the local church at night where she prayed, cleaned the sanctuary, and arranged the altar flowers. The host would sustain her for almost one full day. At the end of each 24-hour period, she could feel her life ebbing. Receiving the Eucharist again restored her strength. Several times over the years, diocesan officials, doctors, and scientists thoroughly examined Therese's life. They always concluded that the only thing keeping her alive was Holy Communion.

These miracles demonstrate the staggering reality of the Real Presence. They also emphasize the immense spiritual nourishment available in Holy Communion.

19 For more details on these and other Eucharistic miracles, see Joan Carroll Cruz's excellent book, *Eucharistic Miracles* (Rockford, IL: TAN Books, 1987).

A SAINT'S SUMMARY

St. Robert Bellarmine (1542–1621) was one of the greatest defenders of the Catholic faith. He admirably summarizes the biblical and historical evidence for the Real Presence:

> TAKE AND EAT: THIS IS MY BODY. Weigh carefully, dear brethren, the force of those words. Surely laws and decrees ought to be promulgated in clear, precise, simple terms, and not obscurely or ambiguously. Otherwise any man might plead ignorance and say, "Let the legislator speak plainly if he wants his law to be kept."
>
> Now what Christian ever doubted that our Lord in instituting this Sacrament gave orders and framed a law that it was to be renewed perpetually in his Church? "Do this," He said, "in memory of me." Since, then, these words of Christ are the expression of a law or command, to read figures and metaphors into them is to make Almighty God the most imprudent and incompetent of legislators. Again, a man's last will and testament should surely be drawn up in the straightforward speech of everyday life. No one but a madman, or one who desired to make trouble after his death, would employ metonymy and metaphor in such a document. When a testator says "I leave my house to my son John," does anybody or will anybody ever understand his words to mean "I leave to my son John, not my house itself standing foursquare, but a nice, painted picture of it?"
>
> In the next place, suppose a prince promised one of you a hundred gold pieces, and in fulfillment of his word sent a beautiful sketch of the coins, I wonder what you would think of his liberality? And suppose that when you complained, the donor said, "Sir, your astonishment is out of place, as the painted coins you received may very properly be considered true crowns by the figure of speech called metonymy", would not everybody feel that he was making fun of you and your picture?
>
> Now our Lord promised to give us his flesh for our food. The bread which I shall give you, he said, is my flesh for the life of the world. If you argue that the bread may be looked on as a figure of his flesh, you are arguing like the prince, and making a mockery of God's promises. A wonderful gift indeed that would be, in which Eternal Wisdom, Truth, Justice, and Goodness deceived us, its helpless pensioners, and turned our dearest hopes to derision.
>
> That I may show you how just and righteous is the position we hold, let us suppose that the last day has come and that our doctrine of the Eucharist turns out to be false and absurd. If Our Lord now asks us reproachfully: "Why did ye believe thus of my Sacrament? Why did ye adore the host?" may we not safely answer him: "Yea, Lord, if we were wrong in this, it was you who deceived us. We heard your word, *This is my Body*, and was it a crime for us to believe you? We were confirmed in our mistake by a multitude of signs and wonders which could have had you only for their author. Your Church with one voice cried out to us that we were right, and in believing as we did we but followed in the footsteps of all your saints and holy ones...."[20]

> **Metonymy**: calling one thing by the name of another; for example: "the White House said..." instead of "the President said..."

---

20 James Brodrick, S.J., *Robert Bellarmine: Saint and Scholar* (Westminster, MD: Newman Press, 1961), 37–38.

This last argument is most compelling. It is similar to Pascal's "wager" that God exists. Bellarmine points out that we really can't lose by believing in the Real Presence. If we believe it, and it turns out to be *true*, we win. If we believe it, and it turns out to be *false*, we still win, for we have a perfect excuse: the biblical and historical evidence for the Real Presence is overwhelming![21]

No Christian should doubt the Real Presence. We have the unanimous testimony of Scripture, the early Church fathers, Eucharistic miracles, all the saints throughout history, and all Christians until the Middle Ages. We also have the unbroken teaching of the one, holy, catholic, and apostolic Church. When God has revealed layer upon layer of unimpeachable evidence, we have a solemn obligation to *respond* and to *believe*.

---

[21] The only way to lose this "bet" is if the Real Presence is *true* and, despite overwhelming evidence, we *reject* it. For then we will have no excuses: no Scripture, no Father, no saint, no Christian until the Middle Ages rejects the Real Presence.

I BELIEVE! NOW WHAT SHOULD I *DO?*

Once we are satisfied of the tremendous scriptural and historical foundation for the Real Presence of Christ in the Eucharist, what should we do? We must put our faith into action. We should resolve to do whatever is necessary to be able to receive the sacrament of Holy Communion worthily. Non-Catholics and fallen-away Catholics need to contact a priest and make preparations to enter into full communion with the Catholic Church. Catholics in irregular marriages need to contact their pastor and resolve any impediments to receiving the sacraments.

We need to learn all we can about the Eucharist, so we can appreciate it more fully, receive it more fruitfully, and pass our beliefs on to our children more permanently. We should go to Mass often, daily if possible, and show by example our faith in the Real Presence. We need to genuflect reverently before the tabernacle, adore attentively at the consecration, and linger lovingly after Mass to give thanks that the God of the universe has chosen to dwell bodily within us.

By our example and zeal, we need to restore the faith of our fellow Catholics in this most precious doctrine. With our love for souls and desire to heal the scandalous divisions within Christianity, we need to invite all Christians to join us in this sacrament of unity.

> *We need to appreciate the Eucharist more fully, receive it more fruitfully, and share it more effectively.*

APPRECIATE THE EUCHARIST MORE FULLY

We can't love what we don't know. The more we learn about the Eucharist, the more reasons we will discover for loving it. At the end of this booklet, we list some excellent resources to intensify your love for Christ in the Eucharist. The best place to begin is the new *Catechism of the Catholic Church*. Sections 1322–1419 give a beautiful and profound summary of this crown jewel of our faith. Read these sections aloud with your family over the course of a few evenings or a few Sundays. Below are just some of the highlights you will discover.

The Amazing Graces of the Eucharist

The Eucharist unites us to Christ. As Jesus says in John 6:56, "Whoever eats my flesh and drinks my blood remains in me and I in Him." Because the Eucharist unites us to Christ, it also unites us to one another in Christ's mystical body, the Church. As St. Paul says in 1 Corinthians 10:17, "Because the loaf of bread is one, we, though many, are one body, for we all partake of the one loaf." St. Thomas Aquinas calls the Eucharist the "sacrament of Church unity."[22]

---

22 *Summa Theologiae*, part III, question 82, article 2, reply to objection 3.

28

The Eucharist preserves and increases the life of grace in our souls. Every effect that natural food and drink has in the bodily life—preserving, increasing, restoring, and refreshing—the Eucharist has in the spiritual life. With an increase of grace comes an increase in the virtues and the gifts of the Holy Spirit.[23] One of these gifts is spiritual joy, expressed by a willingness to defend Christ and joyfully accept the duties and sacrifices of the Christian life.

The Eucharist cures diseases of the soul by wiping away venial sins and remitting the punishment due to sin. It also preserves us from mortal sin and lessens our inclination to evil. The Eucharist helps us to imitate Christ, to have the life of Christ:

> As the living Father sent me, and I live because of the Father, so he who eats me will live because of me (John 6:57).

Finally, the Eucharist is a promise of everlasting life and of the future resurrection of the body. As Jesus promises in John 6:54,

> he who eats my flesh and drinks my blood has eternal life, and I will raise him up at the last day (John 6:54).

St. Ignatius of Antioch calls the Eucharist the "medicine of immortality, the antidote against death," and food that makes us "live forever in Jesus Christ."[24]

In short, because of His great love for us, Christ gives Himself in the Eucharist so that He can remain bodily with us always. Receiving the Eucharist unites us to Jesus and the whole Church, sustains us spiritually in this earthly pilgrimage, makes us long for eternal life, and prepares us for heavenly glory.

RECEIVE THE EUCHARIST MORE FRUITFULLY

If we receive the Eucharist unworthily, we are guilty of the grave sin of sacrilege (abusing something holy).[25] St. Paul's warning is very forceful:

> Whoever, therefore, eats the bread or drinks the cup of the Lord in an unworthy manner will be *guilty of profaning the body and blood of the Lord*. Let a man examine himself, and so eat of the bread and drink of the cup. For any one who eats and drinks without discerning the body *eats and drinks judgment upon himself*. That is why many of you are *weak and ill, and some have died.* (1 Corinthians 11:27–30).

St. Paul emphasizes the fatal effects of receiving the Eucharist unworthily: (1) it makes one guilty of a grave sin, comparable to murdering Christ; (2) it merits punishment

---

[23] The four moral virtues are *prudence, justice, fortitude,* and *temperance*. The three theological virtues are *faith, hope,* and *love*. The virtues are perfected by the seven gifts of the Holy Spirit: *wisdom, understanding, counsel, fortitude, knowledge, piety,* and *fear of the Lord*. The Holy Spirit also bestows twelve fruits as a foretaste of eternal glory: *charity, joy, peace, patience, kindness, goodness, generosity, gentleness, faithfulness, modesty, self-control,* and *chastity*. The gifts available in the Eucharist are designed to meet *all* our needs!

[24] *Letter to the Ephesians* 20, 2; Jurgens, #43.

[25] "Sacrilege is a grave sin especially when committed against the Eucharist, for in this sacrament the true Body of Christ is made substantially present for us" (*CCC* 2120).

in the next life: "For any one who eats and drinks without discerning the body eats and drinks judgment upon himself;" and (3) it may even cause punishment in this life, in the form of illness and untimely deaths.

In order to receive Holy Communion worthily, we must:

(1) Be baptized Catholics.[26]

(2) Have no mortal sin on our souls since our last confession.[27]

(3) Fast for at least an hour before Holy Communion. This means abstaining from any food or drink (including gum!), except water and medicine.[28]

In order to receive the maximum spiritual benefit from Holy Communion, we should also seek to have the proper intentions. We shouldn't receive Holy Communion merely out of habit or human respect. Instead, we should receive with the intention to:

(1) Be united to our Lord and Savior.

(2) Obtain all the graces Jesus wants to give us.

(3) Commemorate Christ's passion and death. St. Paul says, "as often as you eat this bread and drink the cup, you proclaim the Lord's death until he comes" (1 Corinthians 11:26).

In addition to the proper intentions, we should seek to have the proper virtues:

(1) A lively *faith* in Christ's Real Presence.

(2) A profound *humility*.

(3) A confident *hope* that Jesus will give us all the graces we need.

(4) A sincere *love* for Jesus, demonstrated by a desire to be united to Him and by a willingness to obey all His commands.

Finally, after receiving Jesus in the Holy Eucharist, we should show Him proper gratitude by:

(1) Spending time in His company offering Him acts of faith, adoration, thanksgiving, and praise, particularly in the few minutes after receiving Holy Communion.

(2) Frequently recalling and lifting our hearts to Him during the day.

(3) Imitating His example and doing His will.

The Church obliges us receive Holy Communion at least once a year during the Easter season. We can satisfy our Easter obligation any time between Ash Wednesday (about six weeks before Easter) through Trinity Sunday (the eighth Sunday after Easter). It is a mortal sin not to receive Holy Communion at least once during the Easter season. Obviously, this law is a *minimum* requirement. The Church strongly encourages

---

[26] In cases of grave necessity, non-Catholics can receive the sacraments of penance, Holy Communion and anointing of the sick, provided they: (1) cannot approach a minister of their own community; (2) ask for it on their own; (3) manifest Catholic faith in the sacraments; and (4) are properly disposed (*Code of Canon Law*, canon 844, §4).

[27] "Anyone aware of having sinned mortally must not receive communion without having received absolution in the sacrament of penance" (*CCC* 1415).

[28] "Those who are advanced in age or who suffer from any infirmity, as well as those who take care of them, can receive Holy Communion even if they have taken something during the previous hour" (*Code of Canon Law*, canon 919, §3).

frequent, even daily, reception of Holy Communion. We should try to receive Holy Communion each time we assist at Mass.

PASS THE FAITH ON TO OUR CHILDREN MORE PERMANENTLY

In some countries, 90% of Catholic teens stop attending Mass after high school. How can we make sure that our children's faith will last a lifetime? How can we inoculate them against the snares of the world, the flesh, and the devil? The answer is by helping them know and love Christ in the Eucharist. No one who appreciates the infinite treasure of the Eucharist could possibly look to be "fed" somewhere else.

How do we teach our children to believe in the Real Presence? By using the only methods available: *word* and *deed*. We need to talk about the Real Presence as we go about our daily duties: after dinner as we read from the Bible, during family prayers at night, in the car as we drive to Sunday or daily Mass. This follows the pattern Moses gave the Israelites for teaching their children:

> And these words which I command you this day shall be upon your heart; and you shall teach them diligently to your children, and shall talk of them when you sit in your house, and when you walk by the way, and when you lie down, and when you rise (Deuteronomy 6:6–7).

We can't leave to others the task of educating our children in the faith. Priests, religious, and teachers can help. But the *primary* responsibility for instructing our children is ours. That means we must first educate ourselves. Then we must share our knowledge as we share our everyday life.

Start by reading some of the suggested resources listed at the end of this booklet.

We must reinforce our words with *deeds*. Children are natural-born imitators. They will honor as we honor; believe as we believe. They will also judge the sincerity of our beliefs by the sincerity of our actions.

The following good examples will help solidify our children's belief in the Real Presence of Christ in the Eucharist:

(1) Receive Holy Communion worthily and frequently, daily if possible.

(2) Take the whole family to confession often to receive Communion more fruitfully.

(3) Refer to the Eucharist, not as "it," but instead as "Him"—Jesus.

(4) Adore attentively and wholeheartedly at the words of consecration.

(5) Spend time in prayer and thanksgiving after Communion.

(6) Genuflect reverently to Jesus in the tabernacle when passing the altar.

(7) Make regular visits before the tabernacle with the whole family.

(8) Sign up for an hour of adoration when there is Exposition of the Eucharist.

(9) Make a sign of the cross whenever driving past a Catholic church.

(10) Read stories of saints who died for their belief in the Eucharist.

(11) Invite fallen-away Catholics to come back to the Eucharist.

(12) Invite non-Catholics to Mass and offer to explain the Eucharist.

EVANGELIZE OUR SEPARATED BRETHREN MORE EFFECTIVELY

The Eucharist is also the way to accomplish Christ's prayer for Christian unity:

> I do not pray for these only, but also for those who believe in me through their work, *that they may all be one*; even as thou, Father, art in me, and I in thee, that they also may be in us, so that the world may believe that thou has sent me. The glory which thou has given me I have given to them, *that they may be one even as we are one, I in them and thou in me, that they may become perfectly one*, so that the world may know that thou hast sent me and hast loved them even as thou hast loved me (John 17:20–23).

How are we to become one? The context of this prayer gives us the answer.[29] Jesus says this at the Last Supper *where He has just instituted the Eucharist*. The Eucharist, therefore is the source of Christian unity. As Christ promises in John 6:56–57: "He who eats my flesh and drinks my blood *abides in me and I in him*. As the living Father sent me, and I live because of the Father, so he who eats me will live because of me."

Christ gives us another image of Christian unity in His analogy of the vine: "I am the vine, you are the branches. *He who abides in me, and I in him*, he it is that bears much fruit, for apart from me you can do nothing" (John 15:5). Again, the context is the Last Supper, where Jesus has just changed the fruit of the vine, wine, into His blood. We abide in Christ the vine by receiving His body and blood in the Eucharist. True Christian unity will be achieved when all Christians abide in the Eucharistic Lord Jesus.

If we care about Christian unity, we need to shout the truth of the Real Presence from the rooftops. Many Catholic doctrines are rejected because they are difficult to accept: obedience to the Holy Father, confession to a priest, chastity in marriage, the intercession of Mary and the saints. But this doctrine is rejected because it is *almost too good to be true*: the living Lord Jesus dwelling within human tabernacles in the most intimate possible communion! Not only is the Real Presence one of the easiest doctrines to demonstrate from Scripture, but it is also the most attractive and compelling.

Catholics often ask where they should start when they talk to non-Catholics about their faith. The answer is the Eucharist. Evangelical Protestants have a deep desire to develop a personal relationship with Jesus. How much more personal can it get than to have the living, glorified, bodily presence of Jesus not just next to us, but literally on our tongues and in our bodies? Talk about an *altar call*! It is Catholics, not Protestants, who believe in a sacrificial altar,[30] and Catholics who expect

---

29 Chapters 14–17 of John are known as the Last Supper discourses.

30 Catholics do *not* believe that Christ is re-sacrificed at the Mass. Rather, the once-for-all sacrifice of Jesus (Hebrews 9:28) is eternally re-presented to the Father on our behalf (Hebrews 9:24). Only the Catholic Mass fulfills Malachi's great prophecy: "For from the rising of the sun, even to its setting, my name is great among the nations, and everywhere they bring sacrifice to my name, and a pure offering; for great is my name among the Gentiles, says the Lord of hosts" (Malachi 1:11). Virtually no Protestants believe in a sacrificial altar.

an intimate, bodily encounter with their living Savior when they get there.

If Jesus suddenly appeared at our local park, where we could see, hear, touch, and talk to Him face to face, every Christian worthy of the name would race to see His living Lord and Savior! Yet the risen, glorified Jesus is present everyday in every Catholic tabernacle in every part of the world. Twenty-four hours a day, He invites us to a deeper union with Him in the Eucharist, and through Him, to a perfect union with our separated Christian brethren.

A SAINT'S REFLECTION

St. Thomas Aquinas (1225–1274) was one of the greatest theologians in the Catholic Church. He composed the liturgical prayers and hymns for the Feast of Corpus Christi that celebrates the body and blood of Christ in the Eucharist. Aquinas could not only write to the most brilliant thinkers, but he could also preach to the simplest audience. In a Holy Thursday sermon, Aquinas says the following:

> O marvelous sacrament in which God is hidden, and our Jesus, like a new Moses, conceals his face under the creatures made by him! … Wonderful is this sacrament in which, in virtue of the words of institution, the species signify and are changed into flesh and blood charged with divine power; appearances remain in their proper substance; and, without violating the law of nature, the one and whole Christ himself is present in different places because of the consecration as a voice is heard and exists in many places—continuing unchanged and remaining inviolable when partaken nor being diminished at all. He is whole and entire and perfect in each and every fragment of the host, just as a hundred mirrors multiply the same visual appearance reflection.…

> O how unspeakable is this sacrament which sets the affections ablaze with the fire of charity and sprinkles our home's lintel, on both doorposts [lips], with the immaculate Lamb's blood! What wholesome provision for our dangerous journey we receive in this food! What strengthening manna enriches the traveller! It invigorates the weak, brings back health to the sick; it increases virtue, makes grace abound, purges away vices, refreshes the soul, renews life in the languid, binds together all the faithful in the union of charity! This Sacrament of Faith also inspires hope and increases charity. It is the central pillar of the Church, the consolation of the dead, and the fulfillment of Christ's Mystical Body.…

> O living Bread, begotten in heaven, prepared in the Virgin's womb, baked in the furnace of the Cross, offered on the altar disguised as a wafer: strengthen my heart to be generous, keep it faithful on life's journey, gladden my mind, purify my thoughts!

> This is the true Bread which while being eaten is not consumed… Its power saves and completes the work [of redemption]. It is the source of life and fountain of grace. It forgives sin and weakens the grip of selfish desires. The faithful discover here their nourishment—a food for the soul, whose intelligence is enlightened, whose affections are inflamed, whose defects are purified, whose longings are lifted up… O rich unleavened bread! O hiding place of the highest power! Though what we see is small, what is concealed there is wonderful and excellent. O body and soul of the Divinity— divine being inseparable from both!…

> Let no one, therefore, approach this wondrous Table without reverent devotion and fervent love, without true penitence or without remembering his redemption. For it is the pure Lamb that is eaten in the unleavened bread… Approach the Lord's Supper, the table of wholeness and holiness, child of faith, in such a way that at the end you may enter into the wedding feast of the Lamb… There we shall be filled with the abundance of God's house; then we shall behold the King of Glory and the Lord of Hosts in his beauty, and shall taste the bread of our Father's kingdom; our host shall be our Lord Jesus Christ, whose power and reign are without end. Amen.[31]

---

31 Michael L. Gaudoin-Parker, editor, *The Real Presence through the Ages* (New York, NY: Alba House, 1993), 99–101.

CONCLUSION

With Mary we need to ponder this truth in the quiet depths of our hearts. With the zeal of the Apostles we need to proclaim this truth to all nations. If you knew a cure for cancer, would you remain silent? If you had an inexhaustible gold mine in your backyard, would you hoard the wealth? Or would your conscience compel you to share your precious secret with the whole world? In the Eucharist, we have something far more valuable than a cure for all cancer, far more precious than all the wealth in the world. We have a personal audience with the King of the universe. We have a concrete, bodily connection to God Himself!

> *We have a personal audience with the King of the universe.*
>
> *We have a concrete, bodily connection to God Himself!*

For not only is this doctrine a sure anchor in times of storm (as in St. John Bosco's vision), but it is also a pearl of great price that attracts all men to the doorway of the Church. Remember Christ's words, "I am the way, and the truth, and the life; no one comes to the Father, but by me" (John 14:6). In the Holy Eucharist, Jesus remains present on this earth in His glorified humanity, drawing all men to the Father through communion with Himself. The *best* way to be united to Jesus—the eternal way, truth, and life—is to worthily receive His life-giving body and blood in Holy Communion. There is no greater gift this side of heaven.

HOLY COMMUNION PRAYERS

PRAYER OF ST. THOMAS AQUINAS (BEFORE COMMUNION)

Almighty and ever living God, I approach the sacrament of Your only-begotten Son, our Lord Jesus Christ. I come sick to the doctor of life, unclean to the fountain of mercy, blind to the radiance of eternal light, and poor and needy to the Lord of heaven and earth.

Lord, in Your great generosity, heal my sickness, wash away my defilement, enlighten my blindness, enrich my poverty, and clothe my nakedness. May I receive the bread of angels, the King of kings and Lord of lords, with humble reverence, with the purity and faith, the repentance and love, and the determined purpose that will help to bring me to salvation. May I receive the sacrament of the Lord's body and blood, and its reality and power.

Kind God, may I receive the body of Your only-begotten Son, our Lord Jesus Christ, born from the womb of the Virgin Mary, and so be received into His mystical body, and numbered among His members.

Loving Father, as on my earthly pilgrimage I now receive Your beloved Son under the veil of a sacrament, may I one day see Him face to face in glory, who lives and reigns with You for ever. Amen.

PRAYER OF ST. THOMAS AQUINAS (AFTER COMMUNION)

Lord, Father all-powerful, and ever-living God, I thank You, for even though I am a sinner, Your unprofitable servant, not because of my worth, but in the kindness of Your mercy, You have fed me with the precious body and blood of Your Son, our Lord Jesus Christ.

I pray that this holy communion may bring me not condemnation and punishment, but forgiveness and salvation. May it be a helmet of faith and a shield of good will. May it purify me from evil ways and put an end to my evil passions. May it bring me charity and patience, humility and obedience, and growth in the power to do good. May it be a strong defense against all my enemies, visible and invisible, and the perfect calming of all my evil impulses, bodily and spiritual. May it unite me more closely to You, the one true God, and lead me safely through death to everlasting happiness with You.

And I pray that You will lead me, a sinner, to the banquet where You, with Your Son and Holy Spirit, are true and perfect light, total fulfillment, everlasting joy, gladness without end, and perfect happiness to Your saints. Grant this through Christ our Lord. Amen.

PANGE LINGUA (Tantum Ergo)

Sing, my tongue, the Savior's glory,
Of His flesh the mystery sing,
Of the blood, all price exceeding,
Shed by our immortal King,
Destined for the world's redemption,
From a noble womb to spring.

Of a pure and spotless Virgin
Born for us on earth below,
He, as man with man conversing,
Stayed the seeds of truth to sow;
Then He closed in solemn order
Wondrously His life of woe.

On the night of that last supper,
Seated with His chosen band,
He, the paschal victim eating,
First fulfills the law's command;
Then as food to all His brethren
Gives Himself with His own hand.
Word made flesh, the bread of nature,

By His word to flesh He turns;
Wine into His blood He changes:
What though no sense change discerns?
Only be the heart in earnest,
Faith her lesson quickly learns.

Down in adoration falling,
Lo, the sacred Host we hail,
Lo, o'er ancient forms departing,
Newer rites of grace prevail;
Faith for all defects supplying
Where the feeble senses fail.

To the everlasting Father,
And the Son who reigns on high,
With the Holy Spirit proceeding
Forth from each eternally,
Be salvation, honor, blessing,
Might and endless majesty. Amen.

ADORO TE
(translated by Gerard Manley Hopkins, S.J.)

Godhead here in hiding, Whom I do adore,
Masked by these bare shadows, shape and
    nothing more,
See Lord, at Thy service low lies here a heart
Lost, all lost in wonder at the God Thou art.

Seeing, touching, tasting in Thee deceived;
How says trusty hearing? That shall
    be believed;
What God's Son hath told me, take for truth I do;
Truth Himself speaks truly, or there's
    nothing true.

On the cross Thy Godhead made no
    sign to men;
Here Thy very manhood steals from
    human ken;
Both are my confession, both are my belief,
And I pray the prayer of the dying thief.

I am not like Thomas, wounds I cannot see,
But can plainly call Thee Lord and God as he;
This faith each day deeper be my holding of
Daily make me harder hope and dearer love.

O Thou our reminder of Christ crucified,
Living Bread, the life of us for whom He died,
Lend this life to me then; feed and
    feast my mind,
There be Thou the sweetness man was
    meant to find.

Jesu, whom I look at shrouded here below,
I beseech Thee send me what I long for so,
Some day to gaze on Thee face to face
    in light
And be blest for ever with Thy glory's sight.

GLOSSARY OF TERMS

Allegory: A symbolic representation.

Altar call: A specific time at the end of a Protestant service when people are invited to come forward and make or renew an act of faith.

Analogy: A similarity between things that are otherwise different.

Armenian Church: An autonomous Christian church established in Armenia in the fourth century. It differs from other Eastern churches in professing a form of Monophysitism (the belief that Jesus has only a divine nature).

Blessed Sacrament: The term for the consecrated bread and wine when they become the body and blood of Christ. The Blessed Sacrament is perpetually reserved in Catholic churches in a prominent place, marked by a burning sanctuary lamp.

Coptic Church: An Egyptian branch of the Christian Church that separated over the heresy of Monophysitism in the 5th century.

Early Church Fathers: Christian theologians, known for their holiness and learning, who lived no later than the 8th century.

Ecumenism: A movement promoting the unity of all Christian denominations.

Eucharist: (from Greek *eucharistia*: thanksgiving) The sacrament of the body, blood, soul, and divinity of Jesus Christ really, truly, and substantially present under the appearances of bread and wine.

Eutychians: The followers of the heretic Eutyches (about AD 378–452), a monk in Constantinople, who taught that Jesus Christ's humanity was absorbed in His one divine nature.

Exposition of the Eucharist: A ceremony in which the Sacred Host is removed from the tabernacle and placed on the altar for adoration.

Figurative: Based on or using figures of speech; metaphorical.

Figure of speech: An expression in which words are used in a non-literal way to create a forceful, dramatic, or illuminating image.

Grace: God's supernatural gift that gives us a share in His own life and makes us holy.

Heterodox: Not in agreement with church doctrine or beliefs.

Idolatry: Worshipping a creature as the Creator.

Impediment: A condition or action that prevents one from receiving the sacraments.

Incarnation: The central Christian doctrine that the Second Person of the Trinity assumed a human nature and was born of the Virgin Mary; thus Jesus is both true God and true man.

Nestorians: The followers of a 5th-century heresy advanced by Nestorius (died in AD 451), patriarch of Constantinople. He declared that Jesus was two distinct persons: one human, one divine. Nestorius denied the title "Mother of God," contending that Mary bore Jesus only as a man.

Omnipresence: Present everywhere simultaneously.

Orthodox Churches: A body of modern churches, including among others the Greek and Russian Orthodox, that separated from Rome in AD 1054. These churches accept the first seven ecumenical councils but reject the primacy of the bishop of Rome.

Parables: Short stories and figurative statements that illustrate a moral or religious lesson.

Passover: The first great feast of the Jewish liturgical year, commemorating when the avenging angel "passed over" the Israelite homes and killed only the firstborn of the Egyptians.

Infallible: Unable to err when teaching truth.

Last Supper: The Passover meal Christ ate with His Apostles the night His passion began, when He instituted the sacraments of the Eucharist and the ordained priesthood.

Literal: The primary or exact meaning of a word.

Metaphor: A figure of speech in which a word that usually designates one thing is used to designate another, such "a sea of troubles" or "all the world's a stage" (Shakespeare).

Metonymy: A figure of speech that substitutes one word for another closely associated word, such as using "Washington" for "the United States government" or "the sword" for "military power."

Mystery: A truth revealed by God that cannot be fully comprehended by reason.

Real Presence: The dogma of the Catholic Church that when bread and wine are consecrated by a valid priest who has the proper intention, Christ's body, blood, soul, and divinity become really, truly, and substantially present, while retaining the appearance of bread and wine.

Sacramental presence: Describes Christ's appearance in the Eucharist, where His normal physical condition is hidden under the form of bread and wine.

Sanctuary: The sacred space in a church where the priest and servers perform their duties.

Species: The outward form of the consecrated bread and wine.

Symbolic presence: The Protestant notion that Jesus is not really present in the Eucharist, but that it is merely a symbol or memory of Christ.

Symbol: Something that stands for, represents, or points to something else.

Tabernacle: A special box where the Blessed Sacrament is kept.

Transubstantiation: The term adopted by the Fourth Lateran Council in AD 1215 to describe the change of the substance of bread and wine into the substance of the body and blood of the risen Christ, while only the accidents of bread and wine remain.

RECOMMENDED RESOURCES

The Holy See, *Catechism of the Catholic Church* (San Francisco, CA: Ignatius Press, 1994), 1322–1419. A clear, authoritative, and profound summary of the Eucharist.

Reverend James Socias, *Handbook of Prayers* (Princeton, NJ: Scepter Publishers, 1997). An essential collection of Eucharistic prayers as well as devotions to the Sacred Heart, Mary, Joseph, and others.

Mark P. Shea, *This Is My Body: An Evangelical Discovers the Real Presence* (Front Royal, VI: Christendom Press, 1993). A short, splendid defense of the Real Presence.

Stephen K. Ray, *Crossing the Tiber: Evangelical Protestants Discover the Historic Church* (San Francisco, CA: Ignatius Press, 1997) pages 189–269. An excellent overview of the teachings of the early Church Fathers on the Eucharist.

William A. Jurgens, *The Faith of the Early Fathers* (Collegeville, MN: Liturgical Press, 1970) Volume 1. An indispensable collection of passages from the early Church Fathers. Its superb doctrinal index allows immediate reference to the beliefs of the early Church on almost any topic, such as the Eucharist, primacy of Peter, infant baptism, intercessory prayer to saints, Mary, and purgatory. Volume 1 covers the period from the Apostles to the late fourth century. It is especially useful for proving that the original Christian Church was unmistakably "Catholic."

David B. Currie, *Born Fundamentalist, Born Again Catholic* (San Francisco, CA: Ignatius Press, 1996) pages 35–49. A convert realizes that the Bible clearly teaches the Real Presence.

Louis Bouyer, *Eucharist* (South Bend, IN: Notre Dame Press, 1968). *The* reference to consult for all the tough questions about Holy Communion.

Joan Carrol Cruz, *Eucharistic Miracles* (Rockford, IL: TAN Books, 1987). An inspiring assortment of documented Eucharistic miracles and Eucharistic wonders in the lives of the saints.

Nicholas Cardinal Wiseman D.D., *The Real Presence of the Body and Blood of our Lord Jesus in the Blessed Eucharist* (London, England: Burns Oates & Washbourne, 1942). An out-of-print classic that is worth tracking down. It is a gold mine of brilliant and irrefutable arguments for the Real Presence.

AVAILABLE FROM
San Juan Catholic Seminars

BEGINNING APOLOGETICS BOOKLETS

BEGINNING APOLOGETICS 1:
How to Explain & Defend the Catholic Faith
Father Frank Chacon & Jim Burnham
Gives clear, biblical answers to the most common objections Catholics get about their faith. *(40 pages, $5.95)*

Check out Jim's Companion Audio Tapes...
DEFENDING THE CATHOLIC FAITH in which he shows you how to become an effective apologist, defend the Real Presence and the Church's incorruptibility, and use the early Church Fathers. *(2 tapes, $12.00)*

STUDY GUIDE FOR BEGINNING APOLOGETICS 1
Jim Burnham & Steve Wood
Guides the individual or group through 12 easy lessons. Provides discussion questions and extra material from the Bible, Catechism, and early Church Fathers. *(16 pages, $4.95)*

BEGINNING APOLOGETICS 2:
How to Answer Jehovah's Witnesses & Mormons
Father Frank Chacon & Jim Burnham
Targets these groups major beliefs, and shows you how to refute them using Scripture, history, and common sense. *(40 pages, $5.95)*

BEGINNING APOLOGETICS 2.5
Yes! You Should Believe in the Trinity: How to Answer Jehovah's Witnesses
Father Frank Chacon & Jim Burnham
Refutes the JWs' attack on the Trinity and provides a clear, concise theology of the Trinity. *(24 pages, $4.95)*

BEGINNING APOLOGETICS 3:
How to Explain & Defend the Real Presence of Christ in the Eucharist
Father Frank Chacon & Jim Burnham
Proves the Real Presence using Old/ New Testaments, early Church fathers, and history. Gives practical ways to increase your devotion to the Eucharist. *(40 pages, $5.95)*

CATHOLIC VERSE–FINDER
(Bible Cheat Sheet) *Jim Burnham*
Organizes over 500 verses showing the biblical basis for more than 50 Catholic doctrines—*all on one sheet of paper!* This amazing "Bible cheat sheet" helps you answer the majority of non-Catholic objections. Fold it in half, put in your Bible and never be unprepared again. *1 sheet laminated, printed both sides, AVAILABLE IN SPANISH* $2.95

BEGINNING APOLOGETICS 4:
How to Answer Atheists & New Agers
Father Frank Chacon & Jim Burnham
Traces the roots of atheism and New Age movement. Refutes their beliefs using sound philosophy and common sense. *(40 pages, $5.95)*

BEGINNING APOLOGETICS 5:
How to Answer Tough Moral Questions
Father Frank Chacon & Jim Burnham
Answers questions about abortion, contraception, euthanasia, cloning, and sexual ethics, using clear moral principles and the authoritative teachings of the Church. *(40 pages, $5.95)*

BEGINNING APOLOGETICS 6:
How to Explain and Defend Mary
Father Frank Chacon & Jim Burnham
Answers the most common questions about Mary. Demonstrates the biblical basis for our Marian beliefs and devotions. *(32 pages, $5.95)*

BEGINNING APOLOGETICS 7:
How to Read the Bible—A Catholic Introduction to Interpreting & Defending Sacred Scripture
Father Frank Chacon & Jim Burnham
Provides the basic tools to read and interpret the Bible correctly. Shows how to effectively refute the errors of some modern biblical scholars. *(40 pages, $5.95)*

BEGINNING APOLOGETICS: BEGINNERS DELUXE KIT

Father Frank Chacon, Jim Burnham and Steve Wood have teamed up to bring you this kit. It gives you clear, biblical answers to the most common objections Catholics get about their faith. For one low price, you will be able to explain your faith clearly, defend it charitably, & share it confidently. You get ...

- *Beginning Apologetics 1: How to Explain and Defend the Catholic Faith*
- Companion study guide
- Catholic Verse-Finder
- 12-session, audio tape set

The 6-tape set, booklet, study guide, & Catholic Verse-Finder for one price! $44.95
All items in the kit are also available separately.

Call for latest booklets available in Spanish!
All prices subject to change without notice.